Amazing Grace

Words by John Newton
From A COLLECTION OF SACRED BALLADS
Traditional American Melody
From Carrell and Clayton's VIRGINIA HARMONY
Arranged by Edwin O. Excell

Additional Lyrics

3. The Lord has promised good to me,
   His word my hope secures.
   He will my shield and portion be,
   As long as life endures.

4. Through many dangers, toils, and snares
   I have already come.
   'Tis grace that hath brought me safe thus far,
   And grace will lead me home

5. When we've been there ten thousand years,
   Bright shining as the sun,
   We've no less days to sing God's praise
   Than when we'd first begun.

FOLK SONGS FOR MANDOLIN

ARRANGED BY BOBBY WESTFALL

ISBN 978-1-61780-416-8

HAL•LEONARD®
CORPORATION

7777 W. BLUEMOUND RD. P.O. BOX 13819 MILWAUKEE, WI 53213

In Australia Contact:
Hal Leonard Australia Pty. Ltd.
4 Lentara Court
Cheltenham, Victoria, 3192 Australia
Email: ausadmin@halleonard.com.au

Visit Hal Leonard Online at
www.halleonard.com

Arkansas Traveler

Southern American Folksong

Beautiful Brown Eyes

Traditional

Verse
Moderately

1. Wil - lie, oh, Wil - lie, I love you, _____ I
2. Sev - en long years I've been mar - ried. _____ I
3. *See additional lyrics*

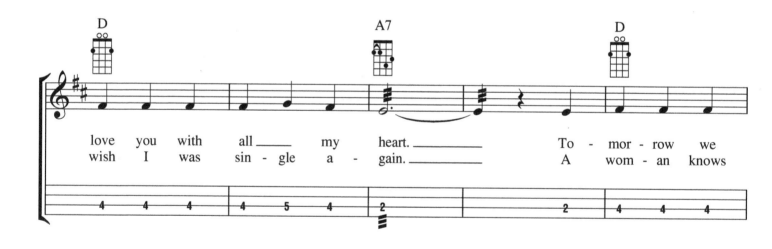

love you with all _____ my heart. _____ To - mor - row we
wish I was sin - gle a - gain. _____ A wom - an knows

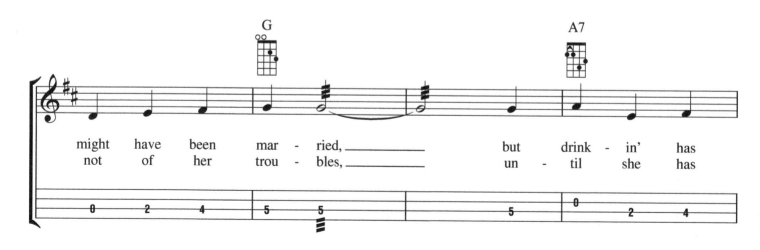

might have been mar - ried, _____ but drink - in' has
not of her trou - bles, _____ un - til she has

Additional Lyrics

3. Down to the barroom he staggered,
   Staggered and fell on the floor.
   The last words that he ever uttered,
   "I'll never get drunk anymore."

The Blue Tail Fly
(Jimmy Crack Corn)

Words and Music by Daniel Decatur Emmett

Additional Lyrics

3. The pony jump, he run, he pitch,
   He threw my master in the ditch.
   My master died and who'll deny,
   The blame was on the bluetail fly.

4. Old master's dead and gone to rest,
   They say it happened for the best,
   I won't forget until I die,
   My master and the bluetail fly.

5. A skeeter bites right through your clothes,
   A hornet strikes you on the nose,
   The bees may get you passing by,
   But oh, much worse, the bluetail fly.

Buffalo Gals
(Won't You Come Out Tonight?)
Words and Music by Cool White (John Hodges)

Carry Me Back to Old Virginny

Words and Music by James A. Bland

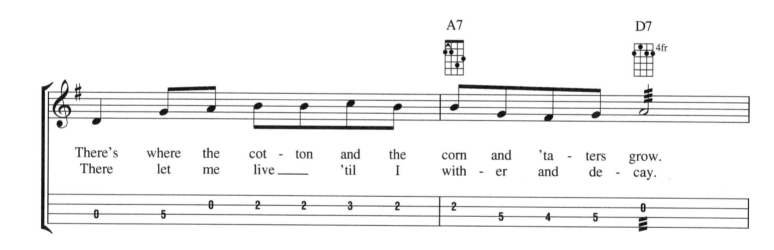

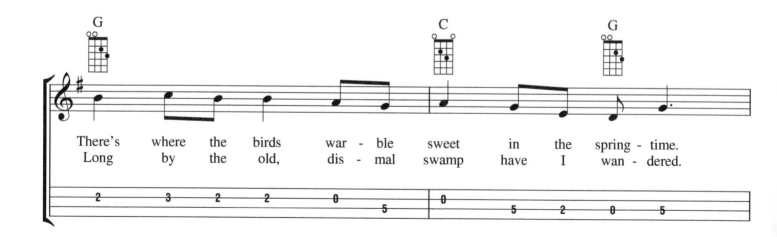

Comin' Through the Rye

By Robert Burns

Down in the Valley

Traditional American Folksong

Additional Lyrics

3. Write me a letter, send it by mail.
Send it in care of Birmingham jail.
Birmingham jailhouse, Birmingham jail,
Send it in care of Birmingham jail.

The Crawdad Song

Traditional

1. You get a line and I'll get a pole, _____
2. Get up, _____ old man, you slept _____ too late,
3.-5. *See additional lyrics*

hon - ey. _____ You get a line and
hon - ey. _____ Get up, _____ old man,

I'll get a pole, _____ babe. _____
you slept _____ too late, babe. _____

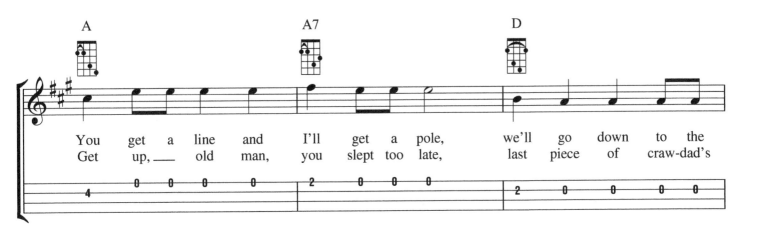

You get a line and   I'll get a pole,   we'll go down to the
Get up, __ old man,   you slept too late,   last piece of craw-dad's

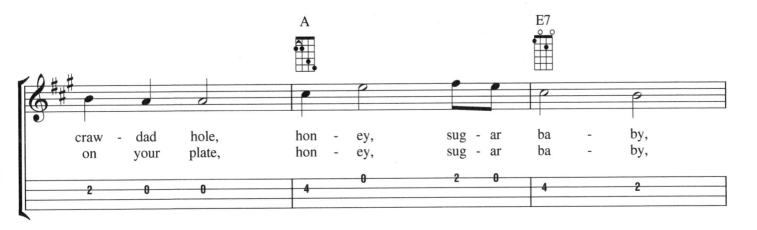

craw - dad   hole,   hon - ey,   sug - ar ba - by,
on your   plate,   hon - ey,   sug - ar ba - by,

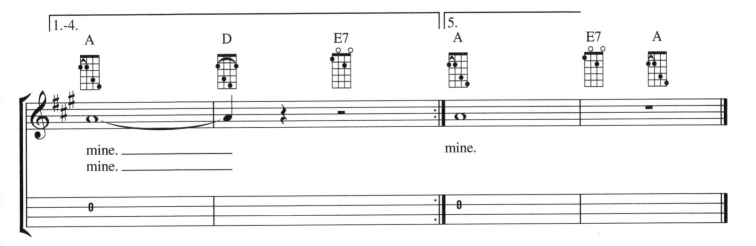

1.-4.
mine. _____
mine. _____

5.
mine.

Additional Lyrics

3. Get up, old woman, you slept too late, honey.
   Get up, old woman you slept too late, babe.
   Get up, old woman you slept too late;
   Crawdad man done passed your gate, honey, sugar baby, mine.

4. Along come a man with a sack on his back, honey.
   Along come a man with a sack on his back, babe.
   Along come a man with a sack on his back,
   Packin' all the crawdads he can pack, honey, sugar baby, mine.

5. What you gonna do when the lake goes dry, honey.
   What you gonna do when the lake goes dry, babe?
   What you gonna do when the lake goes dry?
   Sit on the bank and watch the crawdads die, honey, sugar baby, mine.

(I Wish I Was In)
Dixie

Words and Music by Daniel Decatur Emmett

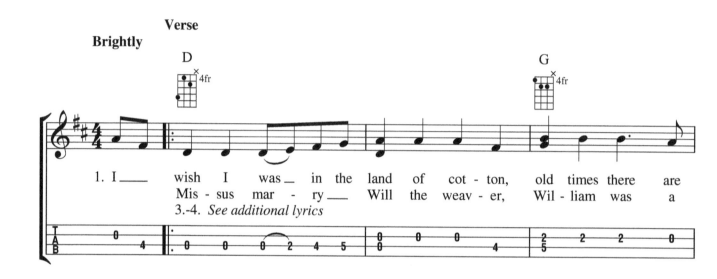

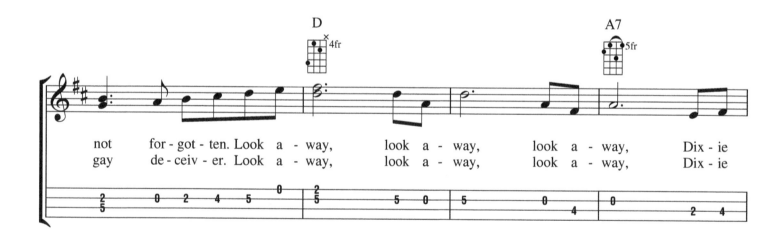

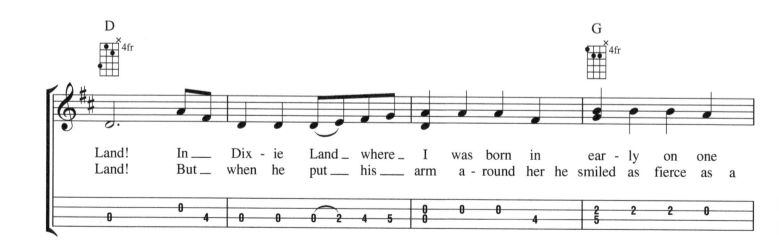

Additional Lyrics

3. His face was sharp as a butcher's cleaver,
   But that did not seem to grieve her.
   Look away, look away,
   Look away, Dixie Land!
   Old Missus acted the foolish part
   And died for a man that broke her heart.
   Look away, look away,
   Look away, Dixie Land!

4. Now here's a health to the next old Missus
   And all the girls that want to kiss us.
   Look away, look away,
   Look away, Dixie Land!
   But if you want to drive away the sorrow,
   Come and hear this song tomorrow.
   Look away, look away,
   Look away, Dixie Land!

Down by the Riverside

African American Spiritual

Additional Lyrics

3. Gonna try on my long white robe
   Down by the riverside,
   Down by the riverside,
   Down by the riverside.
   Gonna try on my long white robe
   Down by the riverside,
   And study war no more.

Freight Train

Words and Music by Elizabeth Cotten

Additional Lyrics

3. When I die, Lord, bury me deep,
   Way down on old Chestnut Street.
   So I can hear old Number Nine
   As she comes rolling by.

Give Me That Old Time Religion

Traditional

Good Night Ladies

Words by E.P. Christy
Traditional Music

Good night, la - dies. _ Good night, la - dies! _ Good night,

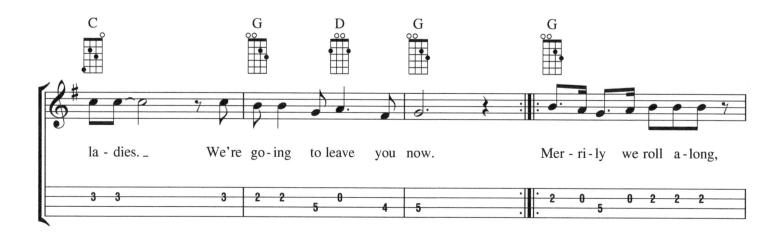

la - dies. _ We're go - ing to leave you now. Mer - ri - ly we roll a - long,

roll a - long, roll a - long. Mer - ri - ly we roll a - long, o'er the deep blue sea.

Hail, Hail, the Gang's All Here

Words by D.A. Esrom
Music by Theodore F. Morse and Arthur Sullivan

Moderately

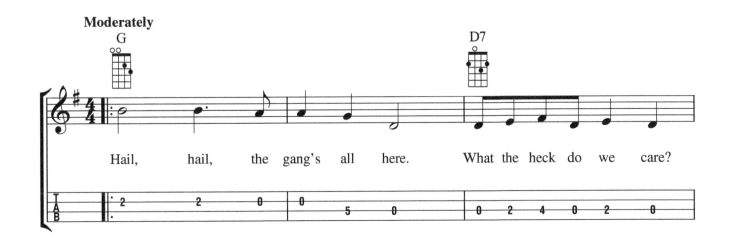

Hail, hail, the gang's all here. What the heck do we care?

What the heck do we care? Hail, hail, the

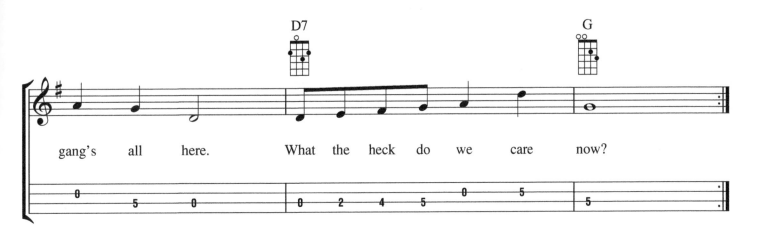

gang's all here. What the heck do we care now?

Home on the Range

Lyrics by Dr. Brewster Higley
Music by Dan Kelly

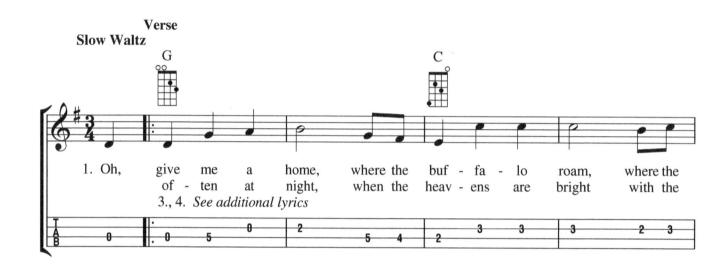

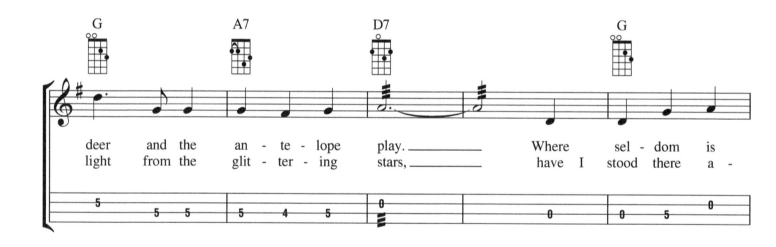

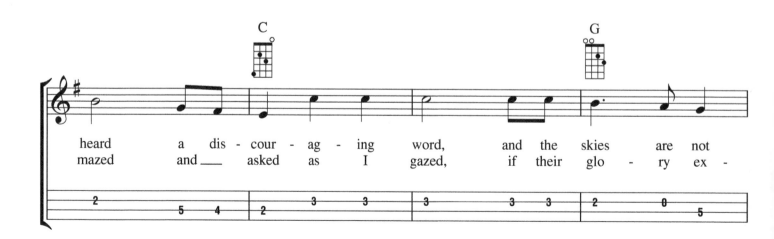

Additional Lyrics

3. Where the air is so pure, the zephyrs so free,
   The breezes so balmy and light,
   That I would not exchange my home on the range
   For all of the cities so bright.

4. Oh, I love those wild flow'rs in this dear land of ours.
   The curlew, I love to hear scream.
   And I love the white rocks and the antelope flocks,
   That graze on the mountaintops green.

Home Sweet Home

Words by John Howard Payne
Music by Henry R. Bishop

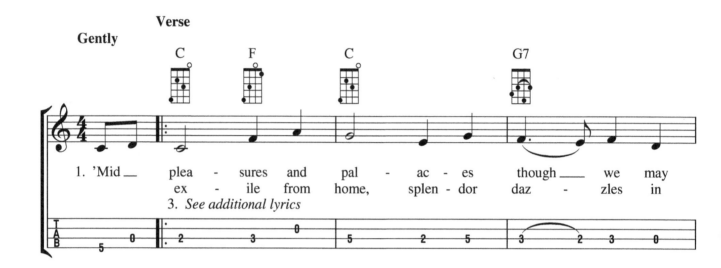

Verse
Gently

1. 'Mid __ plea - sures and pal - ac - es though __ we may
    ex - ile from home, splen - dor daz - zles in
3. *See additional lyrics*

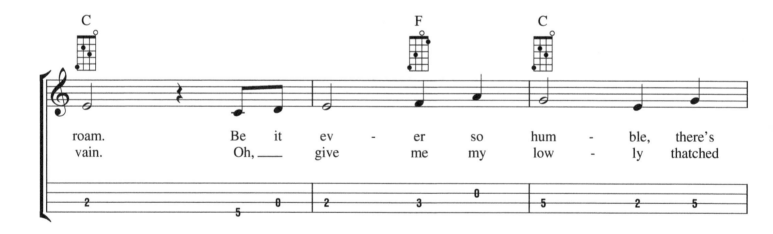

roam.   Be it ev - er so hum - ble, there's
vain.   Oh, __ give me my low - ly thatched

no __ place like home.   A charm __ from the sky seems to
cot - tage a - gain.   The birds __ sing - ing gai - ly, that

Additional Lyrics

3. To thee, I'll return, overburdened with care,
The heart's dearest solace will smile on me there.
No more from that cottage again will I roam,
Be it ever so humble, there's no place like home.

I've Been Working on the Railroad

American Folksong

I've been work-ing on the rail - road, all the live - long day.

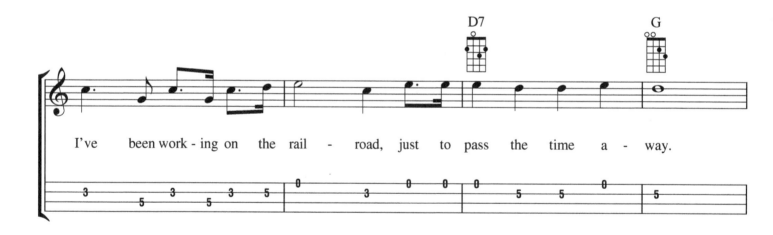

I've been work-ing on the rail - road, just to pass the time a - way.

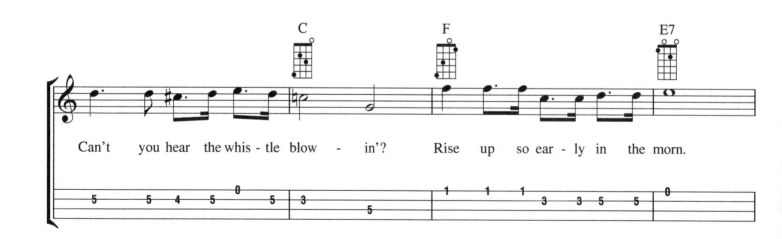

Can't you hear the whis - tle blow - in'? Rise up so ear - ly in the morn.

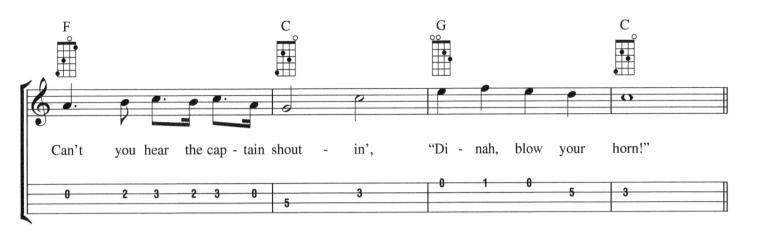

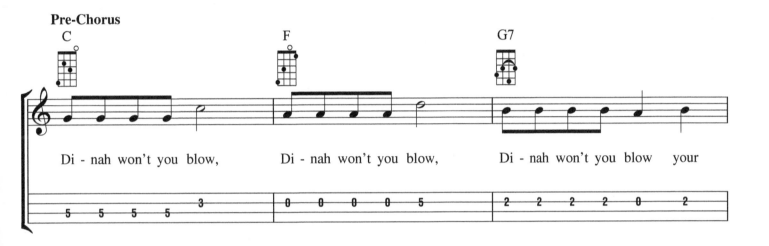

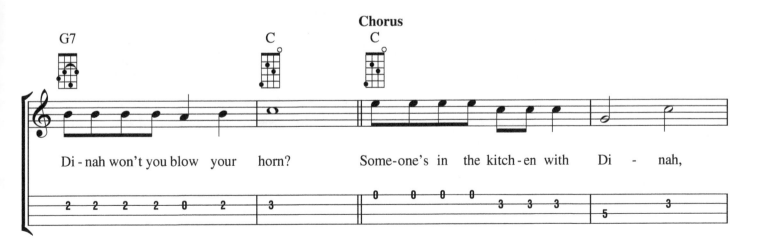

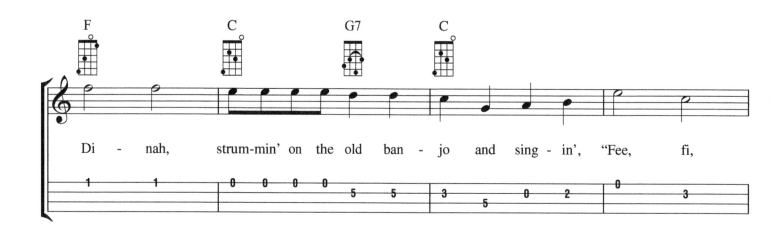

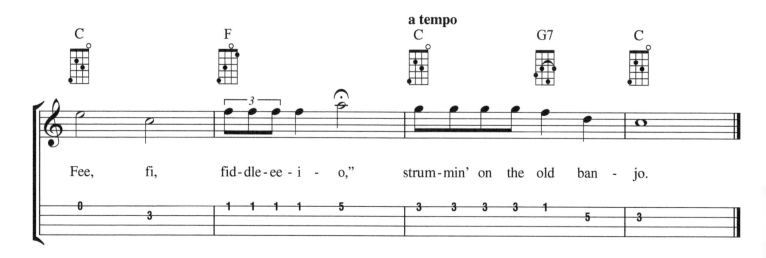

In the Good Old Summertime

Words by Ren Shields
Music by George Evans

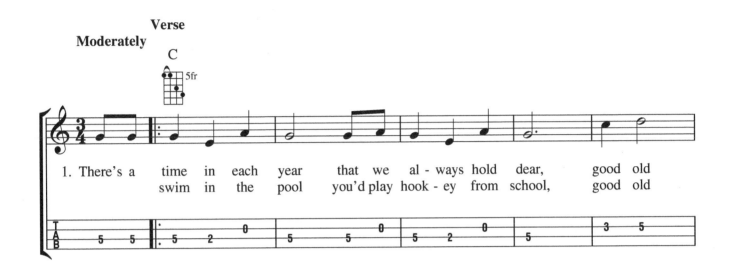

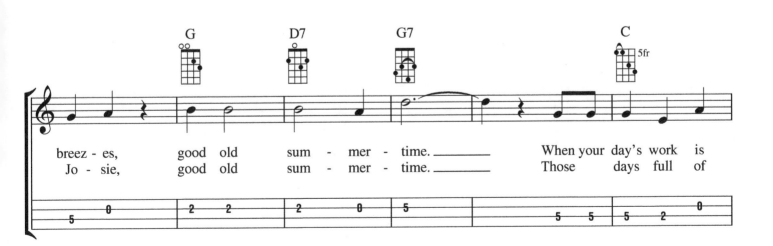

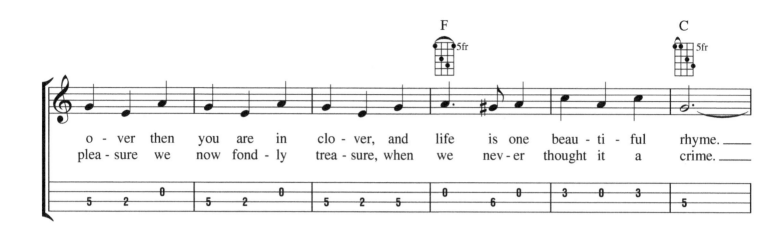

o - ver then you are in clo - ver, and life is one beau - ti - ful rhyme._____
plea - sure we now fond - ly trea - sure, when we nev - er thought it a crime._____

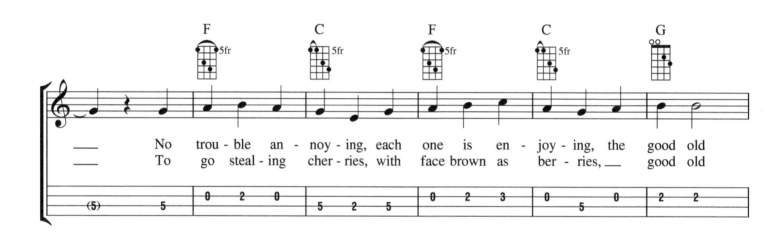

_____ No trou - ble an - noy - ing, each one is en - joy - ing, the good old
_____ To go steal - ing cher - ries, with face brown as ber - ries, ___ good old

Chorus

sum - mer - time. _____
sum - mer - time. _____   In the good old sum - mer - time, _____

___ in the good old sum - mer - time, _____ stroll - ing

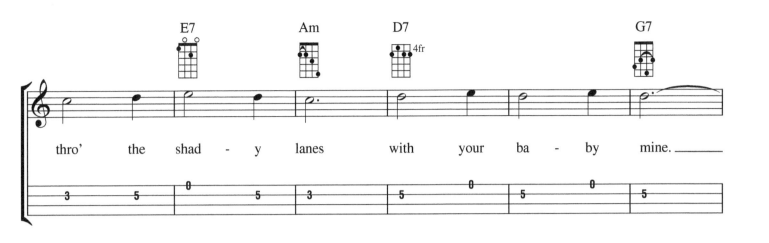

thro' the shad - y lanes with your ba - by mine. _____

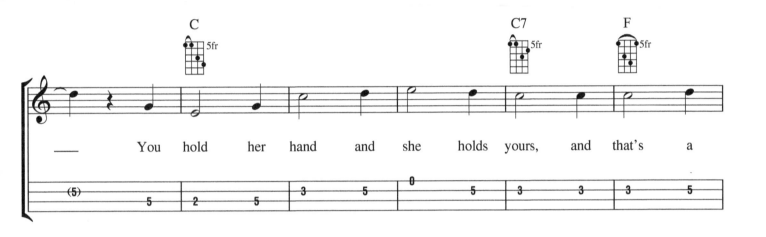

_____ You hold her hand and she holds yours, and that's a

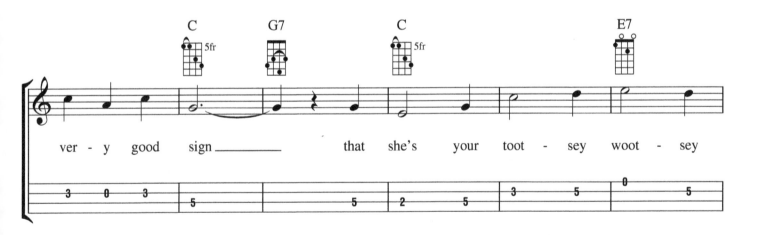

ver - y good sign _____ that she's your toot - sey woot - sey

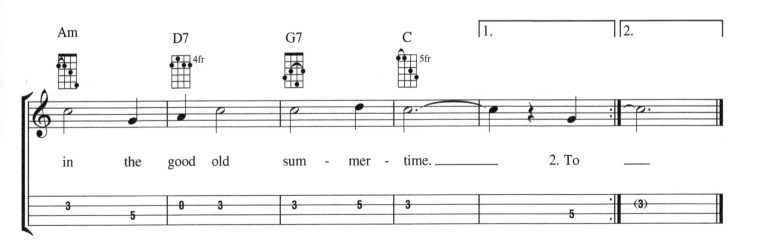

in the good old sum - mer - time. _____ 2. To _____

John Brown's Body

Traditional

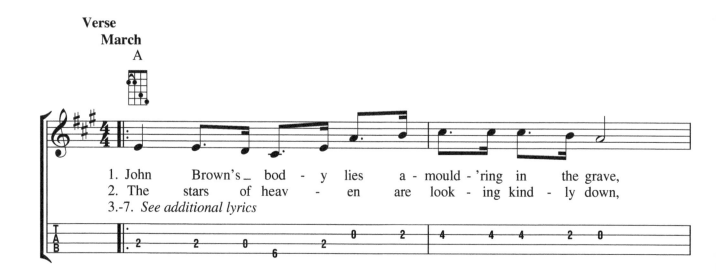

1. John Brown's_ bod - y lies a - mould - 'ring in the grave,
2. The stars of heav - en are look - ing kind - ly down,
3.-7. *See additional lyrics*

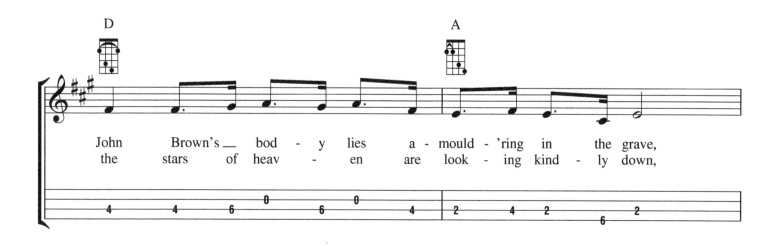

John Brown's_ bod - y lies a - mould - 'ring in the grave,
the stars of heav - en are look - ing kind - ly down,

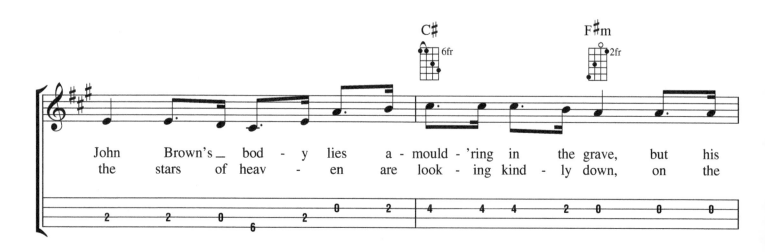

John Brown's_ bod - y lies a - mould - 'ring in the grave, but his
the stars of heav - en are look - ing kind - ly down, on the

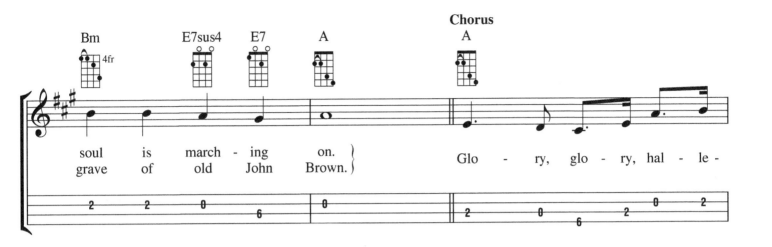

Additional Lyrics

3. He's gone to be a soldier in the army of the Lord,
   He's gone to be a soldier in the army of the Lord,
   He's gone to be a soldier in the army of the Lord,
   His soul is marching on.

4. John Brown died that the slave might be free,
   John Brown died that the slave might be free,
   John Brown died that the slave might be free,
   But his soul goes marching on.

5. John Brown's knapsack is strapped to his back,
   John Brown's knapsack is strapped to his back,
   John Brown's knapsack is strapped to his back,
   His soul is marching on.

6. His pet lambs will meet on the way,
   His pet lambs will meet on the way,
   His pet lambs will meet on the way,
   And they'll go marching on.

7. They will hang Jeff Davis on a sour apple tree,
   They will hang Jeff Davis on a sour apple tree,
   They will hang Jeff Davis on a sour apple tree,
   As they go marching on.

John Henry

West Virginia Folksong

Moderately fast

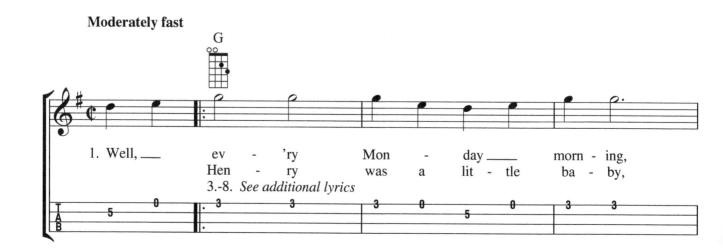

1. Well, ___ ev - 'ry Mon - day ___ morn - ing,
Hen - ry was a lit - tle ba - by,
3.-8. *See additional lyrics*

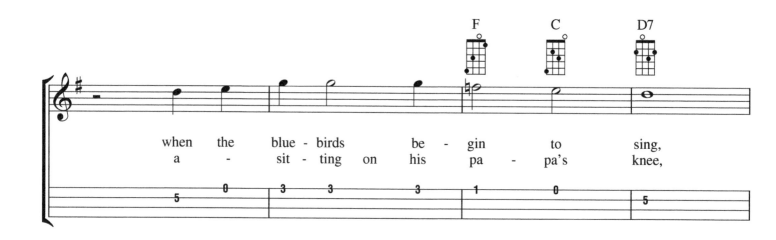

when the blue - birds be - gin to sing,
a - sit - ting on his pa - pa's knee,

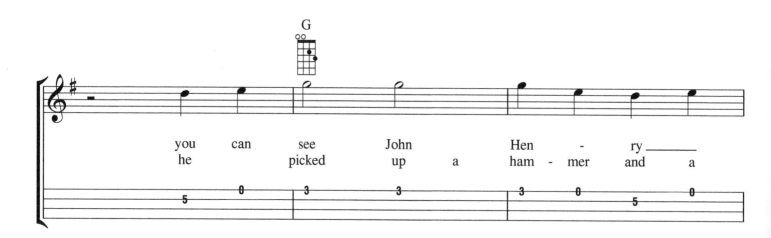

you can see John Hen - ry _____
he picked up a ham - mer and a

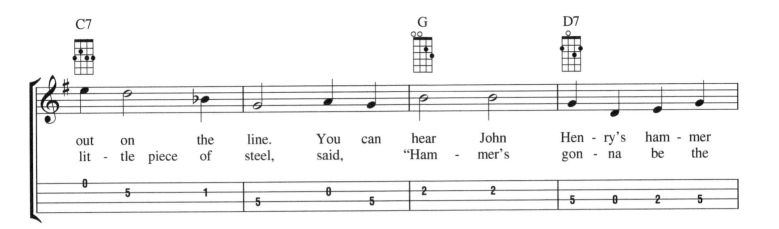

out on the line. You can hear John Hen - ry's ham - mer

lit - tle piece of steel, You said, "Ham - mer's gon - na be the

ring, Lord, Lord, _____ you can hear John

death of me, ham - mer's gon - na

Hen - ry's ham - mer ring.   2. When John man."

be the death of me."

Additional Lyrics

3. Well, the captain said to John Henry,
   "Gonna bring me a steam drill 'round.
   Gonna bring me a steam drill out on the job,
   Gonna whup that steel on down, oh yeah,
   Gonna whup that steel on down."

4. John Henry said to his captain,
   "A man ain't nothin' but a man.
   And before I let that steam drill beat me down,
   I'll die with a hammer in my hand, Lord, Lord,
   I'll die with a hammer in my hand."

5. John Henry said to his shaker,
   He said, "Shaker, why don't you pray?
   'Cause if I miss this little piece of steel,
   Tomorrow be your buryin' day, yes sir,
   Tomorrow be your buryin' day."

6. John Henry was driving on the mountain,
   And his hammer was flashing fire.
   And the last words I heard that poor boy say:
   "Gimme a cool drink of water 'fore I die, Lord, Lord,
   Gimme a cool drink of water 'fore I die."

7. John Henry, he drove fifteen feet,
   The steam drill only made nine.
   But he hammered so hard that he broke his poor heart,
   And he laid down his hammer and he died,
   He laid down his hammer and he died.

8. They took John Henry to the graveyard
   And they buried him in the sand.
   And every locomotive comes a-roaring by says,
   "There lies a steel-driving man,
   There lies a steel-driving man."

Kumbaya

Congo Folksong

Slowly

Additional Lyrics

3. Someone's crying, Lord, Kumbaya.
   Someone's crying, Lord, Kumbaya.
   Someone's crying, Lord, Kumbaya.
   Oh, Lord, Kumbaya.

4. Someone's praying, Lord, Kumbaya.
   Someone's praying, Lord, Kumbaya.
   Someone's praying, Lord, Kumbaya.
   Oh, Lord, Kumbaya.

5. Someone's singing, Lord, Kumbaya.
   Someone's singing, Lord, Kumbaya.
   Someone's singing, Lord, Kumbaya.
   Oh, Lord, Kumbaya.

Little Brown Jug

Words and Music by Joseph E. Winner

Additional Lyrics

3. When I got toiling to my farm,
I take little brown jug under my arm.
I place it under a shady tree;
Little brown jug, 'tis you and me.

4. If I'd a cow that gave such milk,
I'd clothe her in the finest silk.
I'd feed her on the choicest hay
And milk her forty times a day.

5. The rose is red, my nose is too,
The violet's blue and so are you.
And yet I guess, before I stop
I'd better take another drop.

Man of Constant Sorrow

Traditional

Additional Lyrics

3. It's fare thee well my old lover,
I never expect to see you again.
For I'm bound to ride that northern railroad.
Perhaps I'll die upon this train.

4. You can bury me in some deep valley,
For many years where I may lay.
Then you may learn to love another,
While I am sleeping in my grave.

5. Maybe your friends think I'm a stranger,
My face you'll never see no more.
But there is one promise that is given,
I'll meet you on God's golden shore.

Michael Row the Boat Ashore

Traditional Folksong

Moderately slow

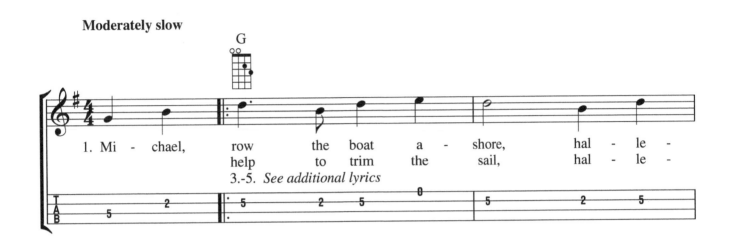

1. Mi - chael, row the boat a - shore, hal - le -
help to trim the sail, hal - le -
3.-5. *See additional lyrics*

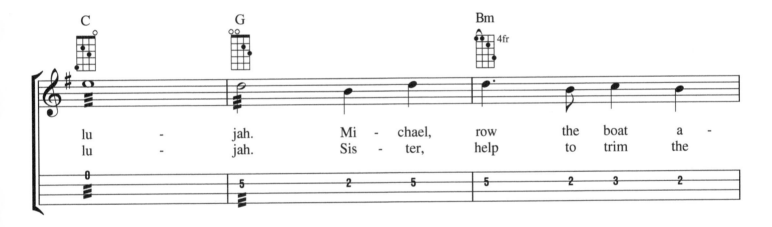

lu - jah. Mi - chael, row the boat a -
lu - jah. Sis - ter, help to trim the

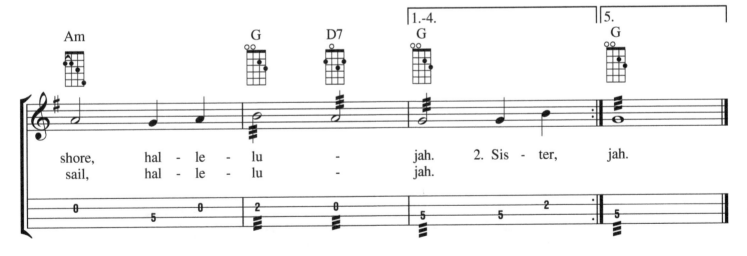

shore, hal - le - lu - jah. 2. Sis - ter, jah.
sail, hal - le - lu - jah.

Additional Lyrics

3. Michael's boat is a gospel boat, hallelujah.
Michael's boat is a gospel boat, hallelujah.

4. Jordan's river is chilly and cold, hallelujah.
Chills the body but warms the soul, hallelujah.

5. Jordan's river is deep and wide, hallelujah.
Meet my mother on the other side, hallelujah.

Midnight Special

Railroad Song

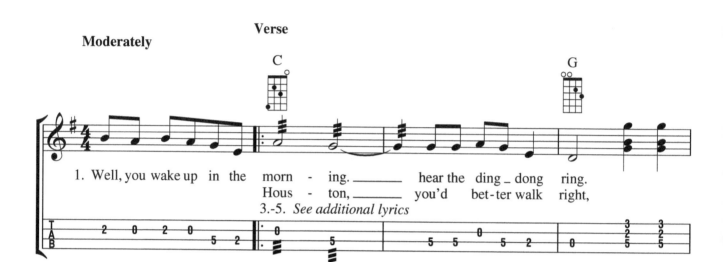

Moderately

Verse

1. Well, you wake up in the morn - ing. _____ hear the ding _ dong ring.
Hous - ton, _____ you'd bet-ter walk right,
3.-5. See additional lyrics

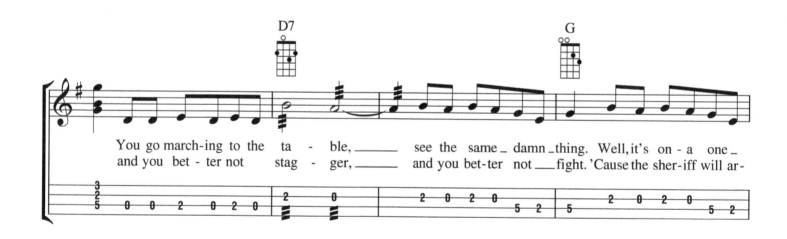

You go march-ing to the ta - ble, _____ see the same _ damn _ thing. Well, it's on - a one _
and you bet - ter not stag - ger, _____ and you bet-ter not _ fight. 'Cause the sher-iff will ar-

ta - ble, _____ knife and fork and a pan. And if you say a thing a -
rest you, _____ and he'll car - ry you down. And you can bet your bot-tom

Additional Lyrics

3. Yonder comes Miss Rosie, tell me how do you know?
   I know her by her apron and the dress she wore,
   Umbrella on her shoulder, piece of paper in her hand.
   Well, I heard her tell the captain, "I want my man."

4. Lord, Thelma said she loved me, but I believe she told a lie,
   'Cause she hasn't been to see me since last July.
   She brought me little coffee, she brought me little tea,
   She brought me nearly ev'rything but the jailhouse key.

5. Well, the biscuits on the table, just as hard as any rock.
   If you try to eat them, break a convict's heart.
   My sister wrote a letter, my mother wrote a card:
   "If you want to come and see us, you'll have to ride the rods."

My Old Kentucky Home

Words and Music by Stephen C. Foster

Additional Lyrics

3. The head must bow and the back will have to bend,
   Wherever the poor folks may go.
   A few more days and the trouble all will end,
   In the field where sugar canes grow.
   A few more days for to tote the weary load,
   No matter, 'twill never be light.
   A few more days till we totter on the road,
   Then my old Kentucky home, good night.

Nobody Knows the Trouble I've Seen

African-American Spiritual

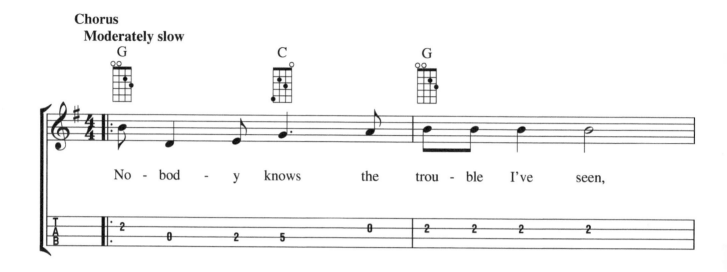

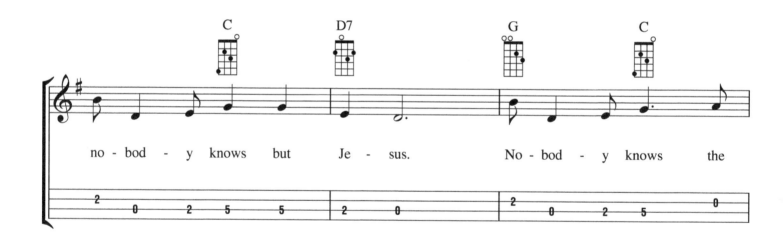

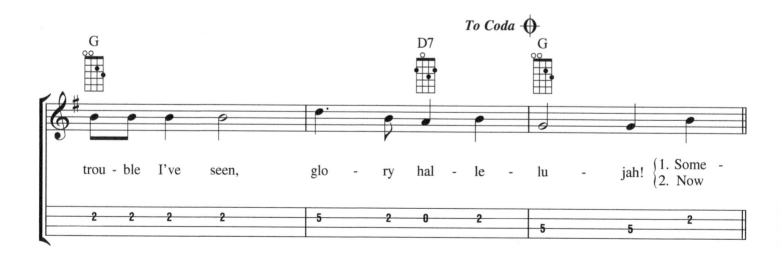

Verse

times I'm up, some - times I'm down, oh, yes,
you may think that I don't know, oh, yes,

3.-5. See additional lyrics

Lord. Some - times I'm al - most to the groun', _____
Lord. But I've had my trou - bles here be - low, _____

Last time, D.C. al Coda

⊕ Coda

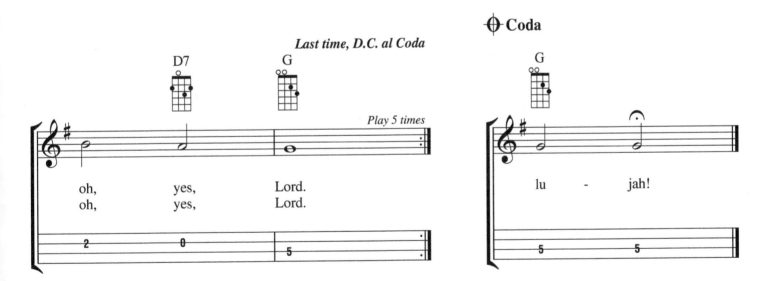

Play 5 times

oh, yes, Lord.
oh, yes, Lord.

lu - jah!

Additional Lyrics

3. One day when I was walkin' along, oh, yes, Lord.
   The sky opened up and love come down, oh, yes, Lord.

4. What made old Satan hate me so? Oh, yes, Lord.
   He had me once and had to let me go, oh, yes, Lord.

5. I never shall forget that day, oh, yes, Lord.
   When Jesus washed my sins away, oh, yes, Lord.

Oh! Susanna

Words and Music by Stephen C. Foster

Brightly **Verse**

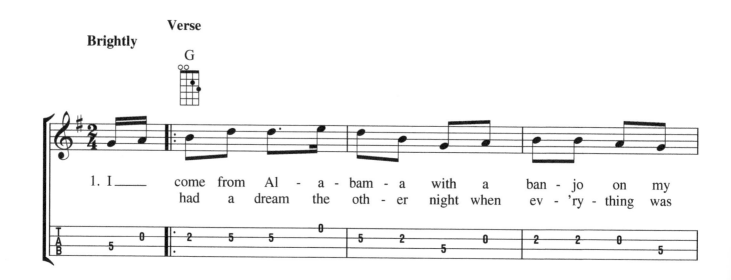

1. I ____ come from Al - a - bam - a with a ban - jo on my
had a dream the oth - er night when ev - 'ry - thing was

knee. ____ I'm __ goin' to Lou - 'si - an - a my Su - san - na for to
still. ____ I __ thought I saw Su - san - na a - com - ing down the

see. ____ It __ rained all night the day I left, the
hill. ____ The __ buck - wheat cake was in her mouth, the

Old Folks at Home
(Swanee River)

Words and Music by Stephen C. Foster

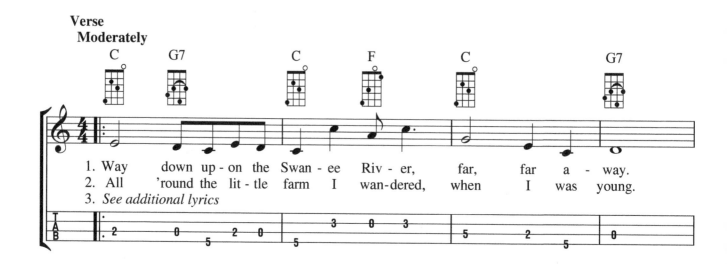

1. Way down up-on the Swan-ee Riv-er, far, far a-way.
2. All 'round the lit-tle farm I wan-dered, when I was young.
3. *See additional lyrics*

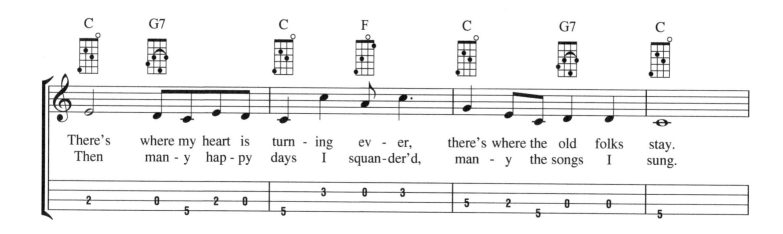

There's where my heart is turn-ing ev-er, there's where the old folks stay.
Then man-y hap-py days I squan-der'd, man-y the songs I sung.

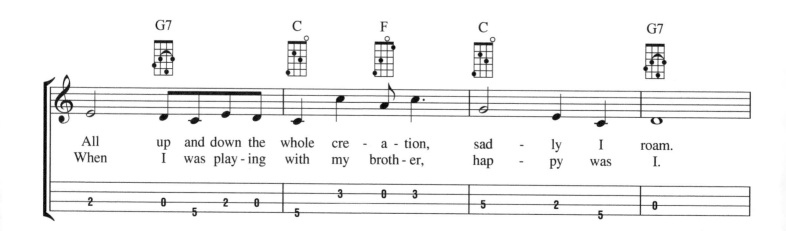

All up and down the whole cre-a-tion, sad-ly I roam.
When I was play-ing with my broth-er, hap-py was I.

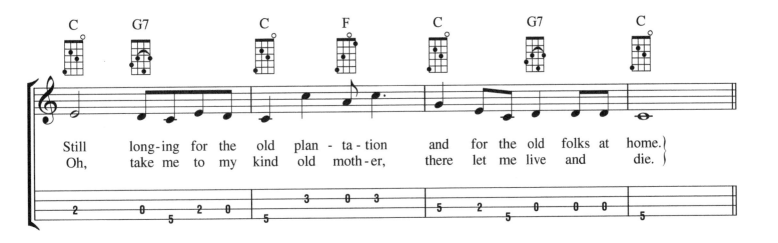

Still longing for the old plan - ta - tion and for the old folks at home.
Oh, take me to my kind old moth - er, there let me live and die.

Chorus

All the world is sad and drear - y ev - 'ry - where I roam.

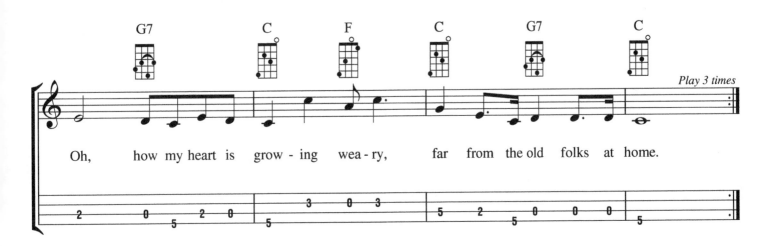

Play 3 times

Oh, how my heart is grow - ing wea - ry, far from the old folks at home.

Additional Lyrics

3. One little hut among the bushes, one that I love.
   Still sadly to my mem'ry rushes, no matter where I rove.
   When shall I see the bees a-humming, all 'round the comb?
   When shall I hear the banjo strumming, down in my good old home?

The Old Gray Mare

Words and Music by J. Warner

Moderately

Oh, the old gray mare, she ain't what she used to be,

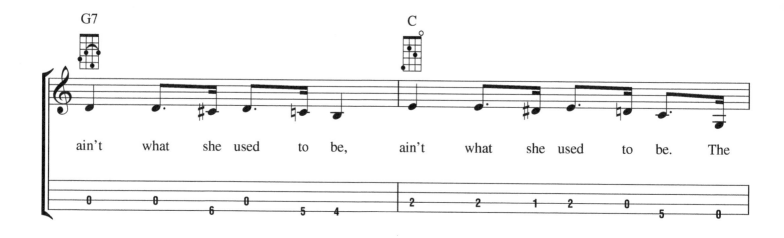

ain't what she used to be, ain't what she used to be. The

old gray mare, she ain't what she used to be, man-y long years a-

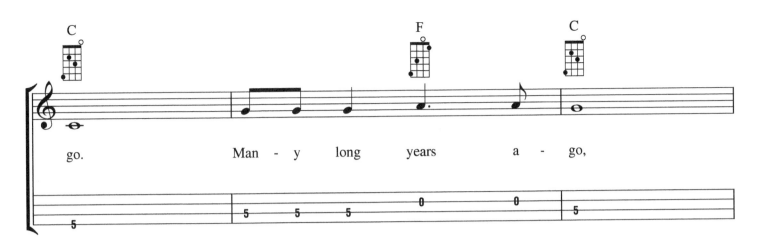

go.   Man - y   long   years   a - go,

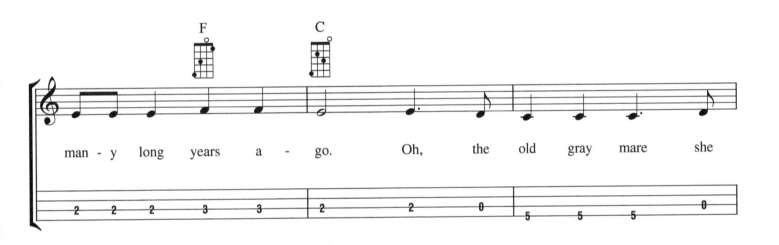

man - y   long   years   a - go.   Oh,   the   old   gray   mare   she

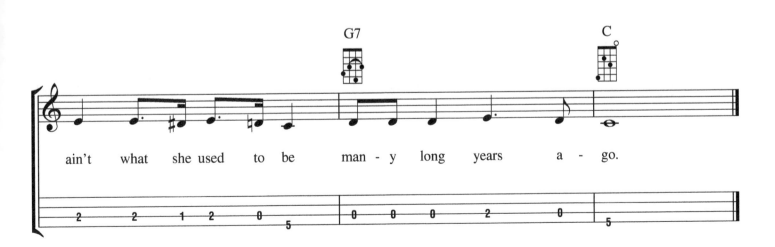

ain't   what   she   used   to   be   man - y   long   years   a - go.

The Red River Valley

Traditional American Cowboy Song

Additional Lyrics

3. From this valley they say you are going.
   When you go, may your darling go, too?
   Would you leave her behind unprotected
   When she loves no other but you?

4. I have promised you, darling, that never
   Will a word from my lips cause you pain.
   And my life, it will be yours forever,
   If you only will love me again.

She'll Be Comin' 'Round the Mountain

Traditional

Additional Lyrics

3. Oh, we'll all go out to meet her when she comes.
Oh, we'll all go out to meet her when she comes.
Oh, we'll all go out to meet her, yes, we'll all go out to meet her,
Yes, we'll all go out to meet her when she comes.

4. She'll be wearin' a blue bonnet when she comes.
She'll be wearin' a blue bonnet when she comes.
She'll be wearin' a blue bonnet, she'll be wearin' a blue bonnet,
She'll be wearin' a blue bonnet when she comes.

She Wore a Yellow Ribbon

Words and Music by George A. Norton

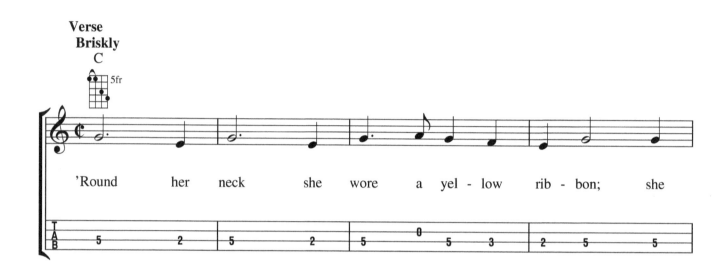

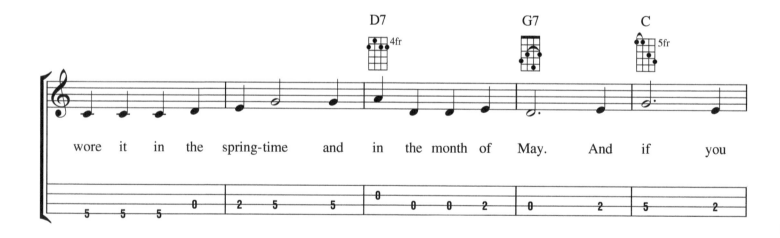

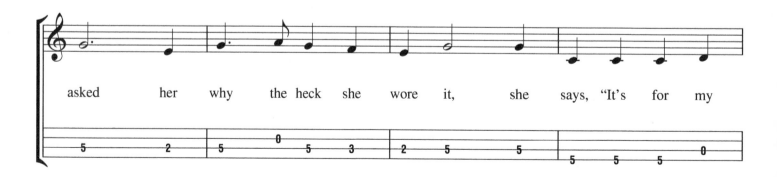

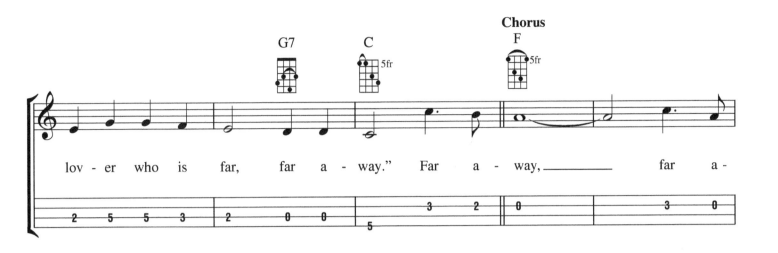

lov - er who is far, far a - way." Far a - way, _____ far a-

way. _____ She wore it for her lov - er far a-

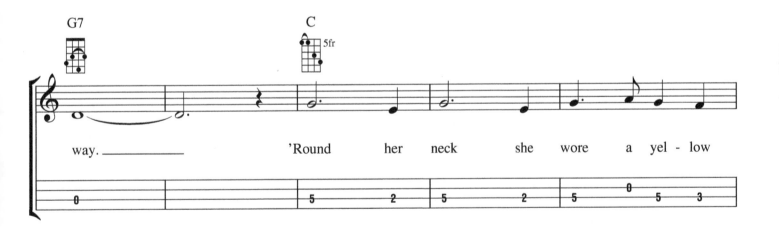

way. _____ 'Round her neck she wore a yel - low

rib - bon; she wore it for her lov - er who is far, far a - way.

There Is a Tavern in the Town

Traditional Drinking Song

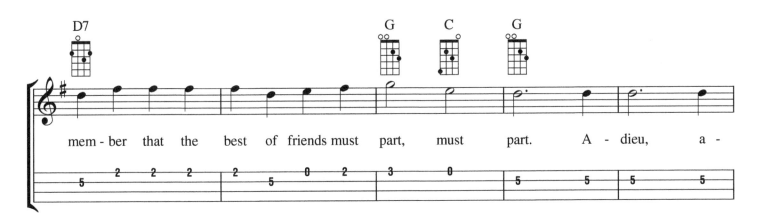

mem - ber that the best of friends must part, must part. A - dieu, a -

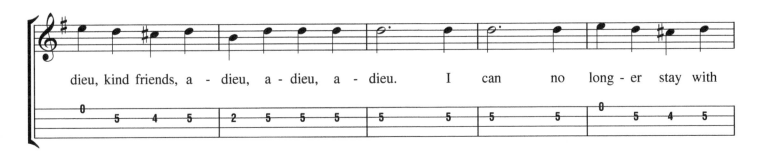

dieu, kind friends, a - dieu, a - dieu, a - dieu. I can no long - er stay with

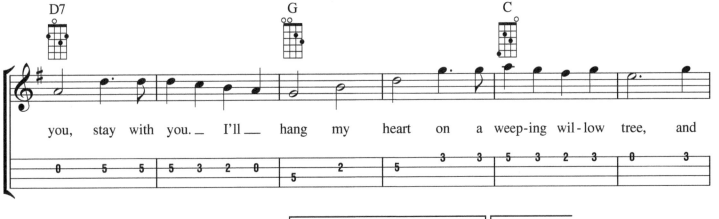

you, stay with you.__ I'll __ hang my heart on a weep-ing wil-low tree, and

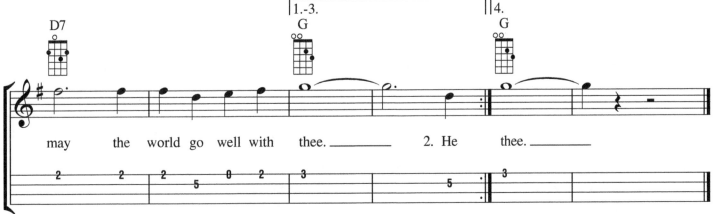

1.-3.

4.

may the world go well with thee._____ 2. He thee._____

Additional Lyrics

3. And now I see him never more, never more.
   He never knocks upon my door, on my door.
   Oh, woe is me, he pinned a little note,
   And these were all the words he wrote:

4. Oh, dig my grave both wide and deep, wide and deep.
   Put tombstones at my head and feet, head and feet.
   And on my breast you may carve a turtle dove,
   To signify I died for love.

Turkey in the Straw

American Folksong

Optional Lyrics

1. As I was a-going on down the road,
   With a tired team and a heavy load,
   I cracked my whip and the leader sprung,
   I says "day-day" to the wagon tongue.

Chorus: Turkey in the straw, haw, haw, haw.
   Turkey in the hay, hay, hay, hay.
   Roll 'em up and twist 'em up a high tuck a-haw.
   And hit 'em up a tune called "Turkey in the Straw."

2. Went out to milk and I didn't know how,
   I milked the goat instead of the cow.
   A monkey sittin' on a pile of straw
   A-winkin' at his mother-in-law.

Worried Man Blues

Traditional

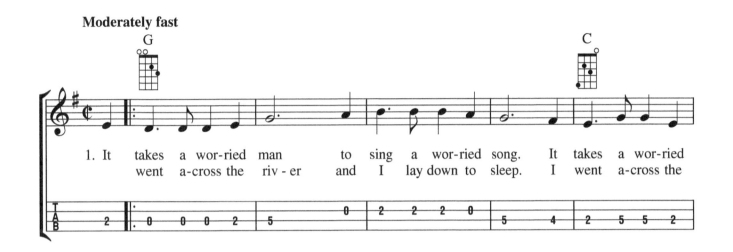

Moderately fast

1. It takes a wor-ried man to sing a wor-ried song. It takes a wor-ried
went a-cross the riv - er and I lay down to sleep. I went a-cross the

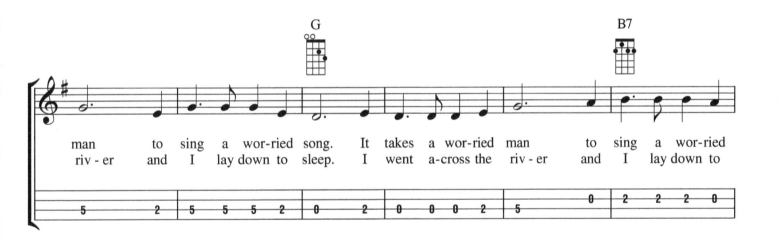

man to sing a wor-ried song. It takes a wor-ried man to sing a wor-ried
riv - er and I lay down to sleep. I went a-cross the riv - er and I lay down to

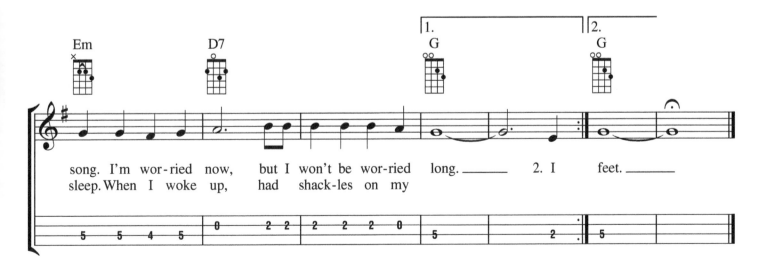

song. I'm wor-ried now, but I won't be wor-ried long. _____ 2. I feet. _____
sleep. When I woke up, had shack-les on my

The Wabash Cannon Ball

Hobo Song

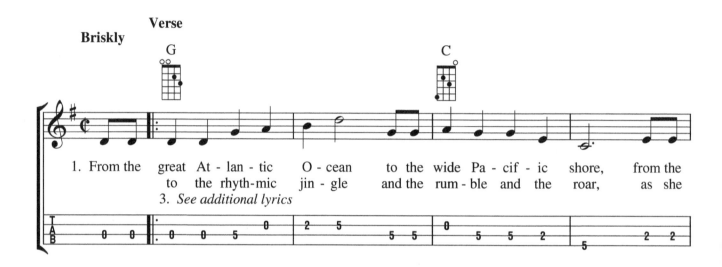

1. From the great At - lan - tic O - cean to the wide Pa - cif - ic shore, from the
2. to the rhyth - mic jin - gle and the rum - ble and the roar, as she
3. *See additional lyrics*

ones we leave be - hind us to the ones we see once more. She's might - y tall and
glides a - long the wood-lands thro' the hills and by the shore. You hear the might - y

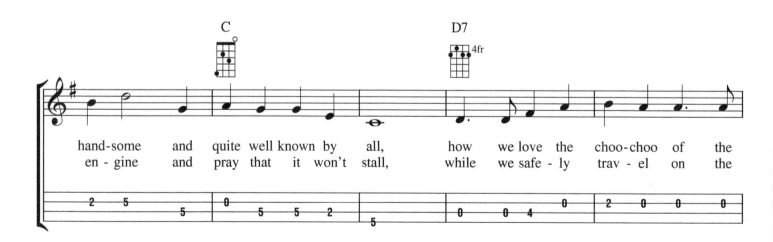

hand-some and quite well known by all, how we love the choo-choo of the
en - gine and pray that it won't stall, while we safe - ly trav - el on the

Additional Lyrics

3. She was coming from Atlanta on a cold December day.
   As she rolled into the station, I could hear a woman say:
   "He's mighty big and handsome and sure did make me fall,
   He's a-coming tow'rd me on the Wabash Cannon Ball."

When Johnny Comes Marching Home

Words and Music by Patrick Sarsfield Gilmore

Moderately

1. When John - ny comes march - ing home a - gain, hur -
rea - dy for the Ju - bi - lee, hur -
3., 4. See additional lyrics

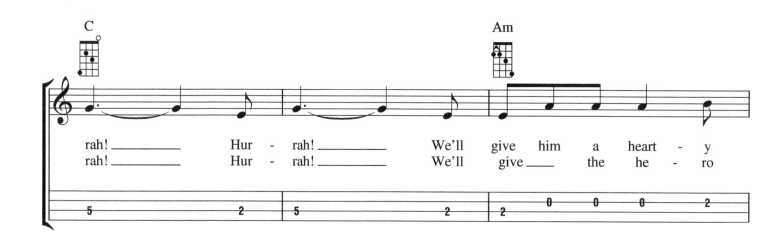

rah! _____ Hur - rah! _____ We'll give him a heart - y
rah! _____ Hur - rah! _____ We'll give ___ the he - ro

wel - come then, hur - rah! _____ Hur - rah! _____ Oh, the
three times three, hur - rah! _____ Hur - rah! _____ The ___

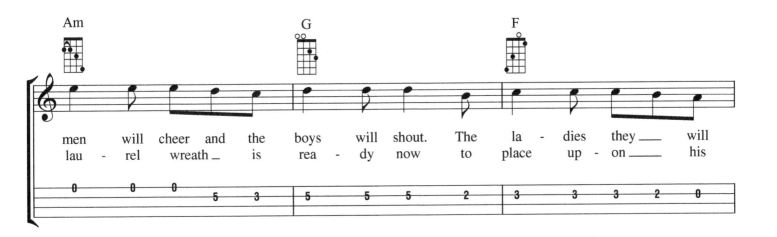

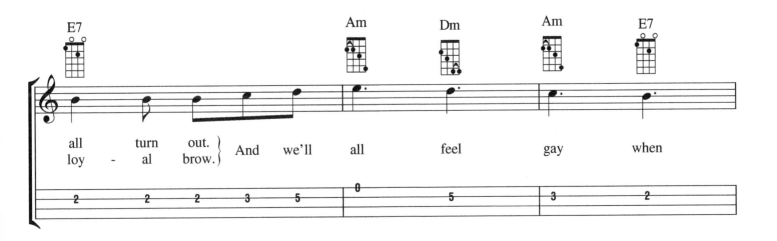

Additional Lyrics

3. The old church bell will peal with joy, hurrah! Hurrah!
   To welcome home our darling boy, hurrah! Hurrah!
   The village lads and lassies say, with roses they will strew the way.
   And we'll all feel gay when Johnny comes marching home.

4. Let love and friendship on that day, hurrah! Hurrah!
   Their choicest treasures then display, hurrah! Hurrah!
   And let each one perform some part, to fill with joy the warrior's heart.
   And we'll all feel gay when Johnny comes marching home.

When the Saints Go Marching In

Words by Katherine E. Purvis
Music by James M. Black

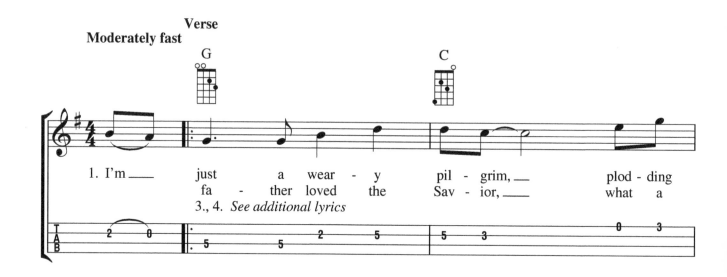

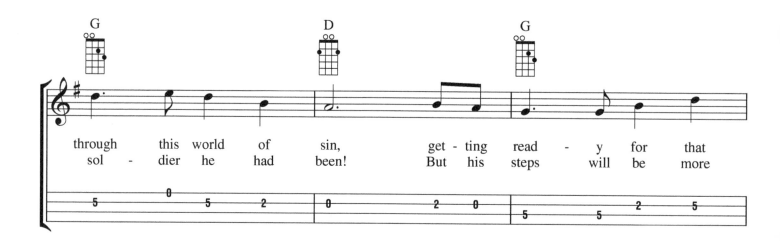

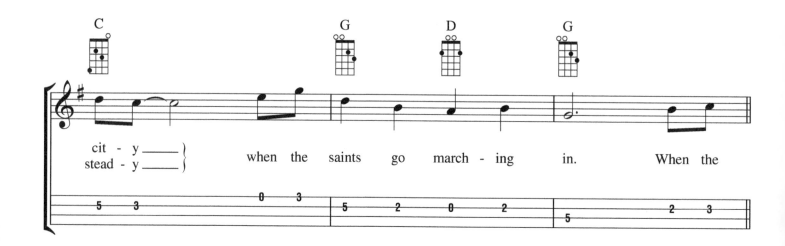

Chorus

saints _____ go march-ing in, _____ oh, when the saints go march-ing

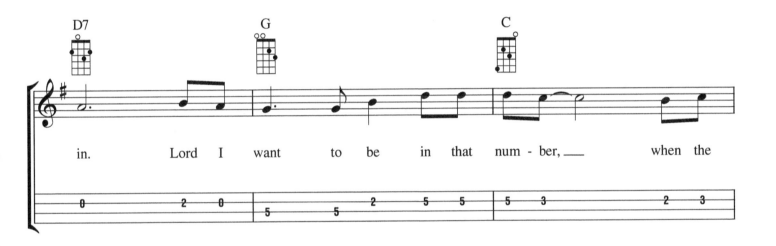

in. Lord I want to be in that num-ber, ___ when the

saints go march - ing in. 2. My _____ in.

Additional Lyrics

3. And mother, may God bless her,
   I can see her now as then,
   With a robe of white around her
   When the saints go marching in.

4. Up there I'll see the Savior
   Who redeemed my soul from sin,
   With extended hands He'll greet me
   When the saints go marching in.

Yankee Doodle

Traditional

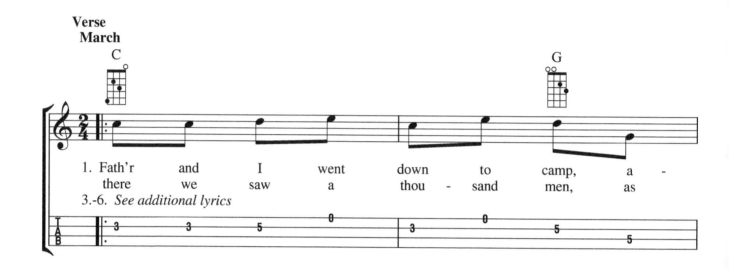

Chorus

Yan - kee Doo - dle, keep it up, Yan - kee Doo - dle

dan - dy. Mind the mu - sic and the step, and

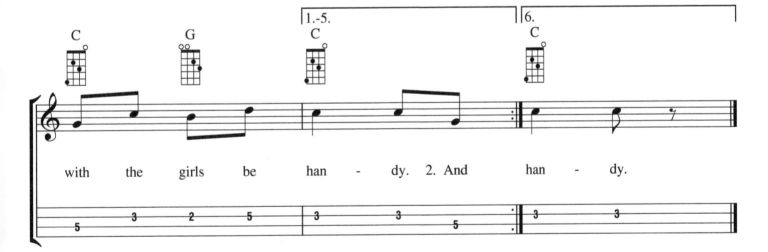

with the girls be han - dy. 2. And han - dy.

Additional Lyrics

3. There was Captain Washington upon a slapping stallion,
   A-giving orders to his men, I guess it was a million.

4. And then the feathers on his hat, they looked so 'tarnel fine, ah!
   I wanted peskily to get to give to me Jemima

5. We saw a little barrel too, the heads were made of leather.
   They knocked on it with little clubs and called the folks together.

6. And there they'd fife away like fun, and play on cornstalk fiddles.
   And some had ribbons red as blood all bound around their middles.

The Yellow Rose of Texas

Words and Music by J.K., 1858

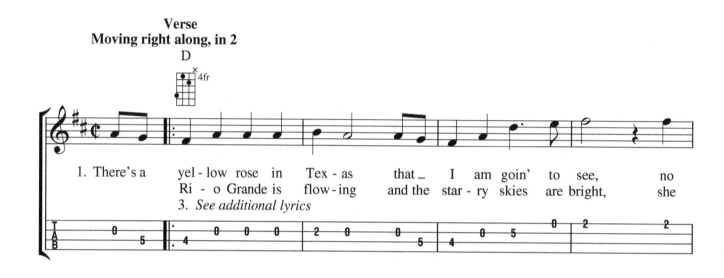

Verse
Moving right along, in 2

1. There's a yel - low rose in Tex - as that I am goin' to see, no
Ri - o Grande is flow - ing and the star - ry skies are bright, she
3. *See additional lyrics*

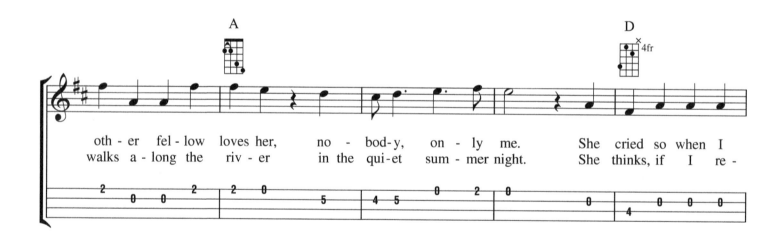

oth - er fel - low loves her, no - bod - y, on - ly me. She cried so when I
walks a - long the riv - er in the qui - et sum - mer night. She thinks, if I re -

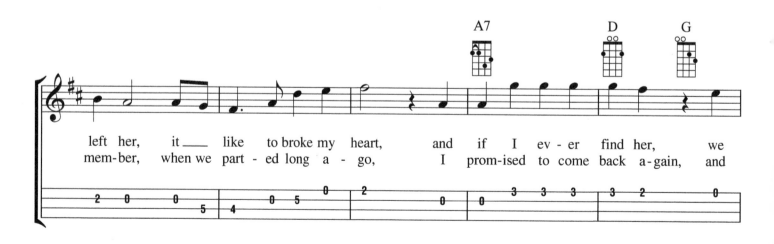

left her, it like to broke my heart, and if I ev - er find her, we
mem - ber, when we part - ed long a - go, I prom - ised to come back a - gain, and

Additional Lyrics

3. Oh, now I'm goin' to find her for my heart is full of woe,
   And we'll sing the song together that we sang so long ago.
   We'll play the banjo gaily and we'll sing the songs of yore.
   And the yellow rose of Texas shall be mine forever more.

Great Mandolin Publications

from

HAL•LEONARD®